בס"ד

UPSHERNISH
THE FIRST HAIRCUT

Exploring the Mystery of Hair

RAV DOVBER PINSON

UPSHERNISH

THE FIRST HAIRCUT

Exploring the Mystery of Hair

RAV DOVBER PINSON

Published by IYYUN Publishing
232 Bergen Street
Brooklyn, NY 11217

http:/www.iyyun.com

Iyyun Publishing books may be purchased for educational, business or sales promotional use. For information please contact: contact@IYYUN.com

cover and book design: RP Design and Development / Rochie Pinson

pb ISBN 978-0-9890072-6-9

Pinson, DovBer 1971-
Upshernish: The First Haircut. Exploring the Mystery of Hair
1.Judaism 2. Spirituality 3. Philosophy

This book has been revised and reprinted in honor of the
Bar Mitzvah of our dear son, YEHOSHUA, *sheyichye.*

Deeply compassionate, full of liveliness,
and wise beyond his years,
he is a source of great nachas and joy to us and to klal yisrael.

TABLE OF CONTENTS

OPENING

THIS BOOK YOU ARE HOLDING IN YOUR HANDS WAS WRITTEN OVER THE COURSE OF A FEW YEARS AND WITH A LOT OF LOVE AND GRATITUDE.

Hashem has blessed us with three boys born one after the next. When our oldest son, Yisrael Mendel, was about to turn three, I began thinking about what exactly is the meaning of the *Upsherin*. What does it mean to allow a little boy to run around with long, free-flowing hair, and then on his third birthday to give him a ceremonial hair-cut?

When our son Yehoshua was about to turn three, I decided to put some of my thoughts on paper and to offer them as a booklet to all who would come to participate at our *simcha*. By the time our Avraham turned three, the booklet became a book, and this is the version you are holding in your hands.

THE FIRST HAIRCUT

My prayer is that you too will cherish the *minhag* (custom) of Upsherin and will come to see its wondrous depths, even if it seems at first to be a mundane or even utilitarian custom. As our sages say, "The People of Israel—if they themselves are not prophets, they are the children of prophets!" That is, prophecy runs in our metaphysical DNA. Thus, any minhag that has become part of the *nachlas ha'klal* / the inheritance of the collective, is founded by the collective 'prophetic imagination' of the people— and is therefore an echo of the revelation at Mount Sinai. This is so even when the minhag is not founded by an individual with prophetic intuition or *ruach haKodesh.*

May you be blessed to have much Nachas from your offspring, from yourselves and from your entire family and community.

Chapter 1:

UPSHERIN

WITH SINGING, DANCING, JOY, AND HEARTFELT PRAYERS, AND A CA-
MARADERIE THAT SPANS JEWS OF ALL RELIGIOUS AFFILIATIONS AND
BACKGROUNDS, TENS OF THOUSANDS COME TOGETHER EACH YEAR
TO CELEBRATE A DAY DEDICATED TO RABBI SHIMON BAR YOCHAI.

Among the throng of people, little boys with long hair sit
perched on their fathers' shoulders. Today is the day these children will celebrate their Upsherin, a ritual to reveal their side-
locks, *peyos*, bringing them into the next stage of life.

Derived from the German word *sherin*/ to cut, and *auf*/off, the
Yiddish word Upsherin, is one of many terms used to describe

THE FIRST HAIRCUT

this ceremony. In Hebrew, the words *tisporet* or *chalakah* are used.

While not based on any Talmudic teaching, the custom to celebrate a boy's first haircut has been around for hundreds of years, and today is practiced throughout the world.

A student of Rabbi Yitzchak Luria (1534-1572) writes that his teacher took his family to the gravesite of the 1st century sage Rabbi Shimon bar Yochai. There, he performed his young son's first haircut with great joy and festivity "according to the well-known tradition" *(Shar Hakavanos, Pesach Derush 12)*. This event took place the 33rd day of the counting of the *Omer*, the anniversary of the passing of Rabbi Shimon bar Yochai.

In the Torah, we find that Avraham "made a great feast the same day that Yitzchak was weaned." *(Bereishis 21; 8)*. The great 11th century commentator, R' Shlomo Yitzchaki, also known as Rashi, writes that this feast took place on Yitzchak's second birthday, as he entered his third year of life. Perhaps this was in commemoration of a transitional moment in the child's maturation.

Clearly, a three year old boy undergoes a period of major transformation at this time; his journey from babyhood to childhood. During this time, he moves from his complete dependence on his mother to functioning as an independent being.

This maturation is somewhat connected to the physical act of cutting his hair; the Upsherin. In earlier traditional sources, there is discussion as to when parents should give their son his first haircut. One source advised the first shearing should take place as early as thirteen weeks; another, two years and others explore the ripe age of five. Today, the most common interpretation is to celebrate this milestone on the child's third birthday. Select chassidic groups, however, perform the Upsherin on the boy's second birthday, upon his entering his third year of life.

In a beautiful metaphor, a child is the bounty of his parents just as the fruit is the bounty of the trees. According to Torah law, *(Vayikra 19; 23)*, we may not indulge in the fruit of the trees within the first three years of their planting. This injunction is referred to as the laws of *orlah*. The word orlah is generally translated to mean "concealment" *(Malbim, Devarim, 30; 11)*. Similarly, the child's hair may be left uncut for the first three years of his life.

To continue the analogy, in the same way that a tree grows tall and eventually produces fruit, it is hoped that the child will grow in his Torah learning and strength of character.

Chapter 2:

THE IDEA OF ORLAH:
BLOCKED ENERGY

THE METAPHOR WE HAVE JUST EXPLORED, THE HUMAN/TREE CONNECTION IS EMPLOYED OFTEN IN THE TORAH. FOR EXAMPLE, "A PERSON IS LIKE THE TREE OF THE FIELD..." *(Devarim, 20; 19).* "FOR AS THE DAYS OF A TREE, SHALL BE THE DAYS OF MY PEOPLE" *(Yeshayahu, 65; 22).* "HE WILL BE LIKE A TREE PLANTED NEAR WATER..." *(Yirmiyahu,17; 8).*

In fact, our relationship with trees runs quite deep. Originally, at the time of creation, mankind's sustenance came only from the fruit of the tree, as the Torah says, "And Hashem said of every tree of the garden you may freely eat" *(Bereishis, 2; 16).* The implication is that mankind was invited only to eat the fruit of the tree, and not to partake of any other form of vegetation.

The connection between humans and trees is drawn on our similarities. The tree grows in opposite directions. The outer, visible part of the seedling reaching upwards towards the sun; whereas the inner, concealed roots burrow into the earth. We too grow physically upward and outward, while our spiritual growth turns inward.

We give fruit as trees do; and the less dry a person is, the more pliable and gentle he becomes.

We will explore the relationship between the first three years of a humans life and the first three years of a tree's. But first let us turn to the meaning of orlah.

In the Torah we find the term orlah used in reference to the first three years of fruit *(Vayikra, 19; 23)*, with regard to the foreskin that is removed during circumcision *(Bereishis, 17; 11)*, and in reference to removing the orlah from the heart *(Devarim, 10; 16)*. In all three scenarios, orlah suggests a covering over, a blocking of something within.

In the case of the tree, the fruit remains closed to our participation or involvement. The fruit of the tree for the first three years remain outside of our human domain; we are forbidden to eat it or gain pleasure from it. The spiritual and physical energy within the fruit that gives us our nourishment remains concealed and removed from us *(Tiferes Yisrael, Maharal, Chap 19; Rashi, Shemos 6; 12)*. Similarly, removing the *orlah* / foreskin is an act of revealing; allegorically, it represents removing the outer layer of our hearts in order to reveal the deeper levels of self.

On a simple level, a little boy with long hair has *peyos*/sidelocks, but they are hidden. By means of the haircut, his peyos are now revealed.

The difference between a pre-Upsherin state and a post-Upsherin state is that in the former, the peyos are intermingled with the hair of the head with no distinction between the hair on the head and the hair growing down the cheeks. Through the Up-sherin, an act of *havdalah* / separation is made. The importance of the process of distinguishing and making borders is integral to our mental and spiritual development. We will discuss this idea at greater length later.

Chapter 3:

THE AGE OF THREE:
A TIME OF TRANSITION

EVERY AGE AND EVERY MOVEMENT OF CHANGE IS MARKED BY A CEREMONY TO SHOW SUPPORT FOR THE ONE UNDERGOING THE TRANSITION, AS WELL AS TO FACILITATE A SMOOTHER, LESS TURBULENT TRANSITION.

Children moving from what can be called a "pre-personal" stage to a "personal" stage, going from non-self-awareness to self-awareness, become very protective of both their space and their ego. When a child first discovers his own separateness from the mother, that he is a distinct person with an individual body and has unique wants and desires, this awareness can be as frightening as it is empowering. The process of individuation, as some psychologists refer to it, begins at an early stage of life, and shows up with a kind of vengeance in the second year of life, the terrible twos, as they are known.

THE FIRST HAIRCUT

When the child nears his third year of life, on a developmental level, he enters a transitional stage, no longer a baby swaddled in diapers drinking a bottle, he is now a boy. He emerges from the sheltered comfort of the home and steps out into school, and is surrounded by friends in addition to his immediate family. Simply, the baby has matured and is beginning a new phase in growing up, from an insular protected life to one less sheltered. Similar to the fruit of the tree after its third year, the child's fruit, his personality, may now be shared and appreciated by others.

To mark this advancement into maturity and to make it memorable, an Upsherin is celebrated. With joy and various intriguing customs, this occasion is meant to excite the child, to infuse him with enthusiasm.

Chapter 4:

THREE STAGES OF DEVELOPMENT

To create the new, there needs to be a loosening or separation of the old. A seed rots in the earth before it can offer new life; first comes sterility, then fertility. Often, the first thing needed is a Havdalah / radical break and separation from the past to move forward in a more rewarding future.

On a developmental plane, a child passes through three stages of transformation from birth until the age of three. Each stage requires its own *havdalah*/separation so that later there can be a greater *hamtakah*/sweetening and re-integration on a deeper, more profound level.

The first and principal *havdalah*/separation in the life of every

THE FIRST HAIRCUT

living being is the process of birth itself. Birth occurs through a great *tzimtzum*/contraction that literally ejects a fetus from the warmth and comfort of his/her mother's womb.

Immediately, a total and radical havdalah is needed in the form of cutting the umbilical cord, as the fetus severs ties with her mother. The havdalah of birth is so devastating to the mother, manifesting in the form of separation anxiety (some are very conscious of the experience, others less so), that the mother becomes *tamei*. The word *tamei* is translated as "impure" but implies a connection with death.

Ritual impurity of Torah law has nothing to do with hygiene of uncleanliness. Rather it indicates a person's involvement or connection with the concept of death. In the months of pregnancy, the fetus is considered *yerech imo*/part of and within the body of the mother herself *(Chulin, 68a)*. So much so, that a father is considered a father from the moment of conception whereas a mother is not considered a mother until the moment of birth *(Beis Ha'Otzer Erech Av)*. Birth is the moment of separation.

The mother, having carried the fetus for nine or so months, with the fetus being part of and within her body, the birth of a child outside the body is a form of death. With the eventual severance of the umbilical cord, there is a drastic form of havdalah. The movement is overwhelming and devastating for all parties, from pre-birth *ibbur*/fetus status to post birth *yenukah*/suckling status, and is thus considered a form of death and renders the mother tamei.

The next movement for the male child is its transition from pre-Bris, an Oral / uncircumcised condition to post *bris*, a *mahul*/circumcised condition, from pre-covenant reality to entering into the covenant of Avraham. For the first seven days of his life, the baby is pre-bris. Only on the eighth day is a child given the opportunity, albeit through his parents' decision, to enter into a transcendent, everlasting connection with his Creator.

Seven represents creation, the cycle of the week. The number seven represents the duration of time, and the celebration of what is.

Eight represents transcendence. Eight is that which is above the natural cycle of time and beyond the immediate; the celebration and anticipation of what could be.

The cutting, the havdalah of the Bris removes the orlah, the covering over, the foreskin, and reveals this transcendent and eternal bond which can be felt and observed even within the physical body. The female child is born post-covenant and therefore does not need a process to reveal the covenant, as our sages say, *"Isha K'man De'mahila Dami"* / *"A woman is like circumcised" (Avodah Zarah, 27a).* Accordingly, women's bodies are innately fashioned to create anew, to bring life into this world; thus they are more naturally connected with transcendence.

The third shift of childhood is the process of the upsherin.

Up until a certain age, children feel themselves bodiless, genderless even, much like Adam and Chava (Adam and Eve) before becoming aware of their nakedness. We all experience times, whether at the beginning of our life or in the midst, when our lives mimic the life of Adam in the Garden of the Tree of Life, when there is complete oneness and integration, with no awareness of separation.

With regard to young children, when they are this way, without

THE FIRST HAIRCUT

shame and with a desire to be appreciated as they are, the challenge of parents and friends is to honor and give young children that space for them to just be, without a definition. For a boy to just be, without needing to be a "boy".

At each stage of the first three years, whenever there is monumental movement, there is a break with the old, a cutting off, a havdalah / separation. From cutting the umbilical cord, moving from within the mother to independence, to the Bris, to the Upsherin; now the little baby is a little boy.

From being a young genderless child, as it were, to becoming a boy at the age of three, parents begin to educate their child in the ways of a Torah observant boy. This is first done by cutting his head hair, leaving the peyos and putting on Yarmulka, otherwise known as a *kippa*/headcovering and wearing *tzitzis*. The upsherin expresses the child becoming a boy, losing the longer, girl-like hair and assuming a shorter, more defined boy haircut.

Chapter 5:

BOUNDLESS & BORDERS: CIRCLES & LINES

SA'AR IS THE HEBREW WORD FOR HAIR. THE LETTERS THAT MAKE UP THE WORD FOR HAIR CAN ALSO BE USED TO SPELL THE WORD SHA'AR/ GATE AND SHIUR/MEASUREMENT *(Ramchal, Adir BaMarom, p. 299)*. EVERY SEPARATE STRAND OF HAIR REPRESENTS A MEASUREMENT, A PRECISE BOUNDARY, A PARTICULAR GATE.

In addition to the boundary each individual hair represents, the act of the Upsherin, the creation of the peyos, expresses even more so the idea of establishing a boundary and affirming a border.

The word peyos is the plural form of the word *peah*, whose *gematriya*/numerical value is 86, *(Pei/80, Aleph/1 and Hei/5 = 86)*. The number 86 is also the gematriya, of the Divine name of Elokim, *(Aleph/1, Lamed/30, Hei/5, Yud/10, and Mem/40 = 86)*. Elokim represents the aspect of *din*/judgment, boundary, order. The creation of the physical world is through Elokim, as in, "In the beginning, Elokim created".

THE FIRST HAIRCUT

In the Torah, we find the idea of peah in reference to a field owner and the poor. Torah law requires that a person who owns a field leave some of the crop (rabbinically, at least one sixtieth of the entire crop,) for the poor. "When you reap the harvest of your land, you shall not reap to the very corners of your field.... You shall leave them for the poor and stranger," *(Vayikra, 19; 9-10).* Left at the edge and corner of the field, the peah itself sets up a boundary, a border that separates what the field owner keeps for himself and what the poor receive for themselves.

Dialectically speaking, the border of peah actually established a separation for the purpose of greater unification. By setting aside a portion for the poor within the field of an owner, a relationship between owner and the people who collect the produce, is established, a relationship that would otherwise not necessarily exist. The border separates to allow for deeper connections.

The charity that is given from the more fortunate to the less fortunate establishes a relationship between giver and receiver.

Ultimately, a deep bond between the two owners is revealed, the person who gives it away, and the person who now has it in his possession.

Tzedakah is generally the Hebrew word used for charity, though literally translated, it means doing what is right. Clearly, there is a marked distinction between giving charity and doing what is right.

To be charitable is to assume that money or belongings are yours, and that you are nice enough to give away your money or possessions to others. Tzedakah means doing right, being aware that the money you are giving to the poor has been offered to you as a gift from Above, to be kept in your trust until you distribute it to its rightful owner.

UPSHERNISH

Suppose you own a field and set aside a peah on the corner of your field. A line is drawn exposing how much belongs to you, how much of yours is in fact yours, and what of yours belongs to others. The peah reveals how much of you extend and spreads out, as it were, over your own belongings and where there is a clear divide, a distinct perimeter where the other begins.

Peyos/the corners of the hair, which are the sideburns or ear locks, serve the same purpose. Peyos on the field and on the hair both set a distinction, a border and simultaneously allow for a deeper connection between the head hair and eventual facial hair, between the child and the people around him.

Peyos are indistinguishable for the person who goes with long, unkempt hair. Long hair, as will shortly be explored, represents untamed, unbridled and unrestrained energy, energy that extends non-restrictively in all directions and places, free flowing and wild. A small baby boy running about before his upsherin, long hair flowing behind him, represents a little bundle of energy, brimming with life and exuberance. It is a beautiful thing for a young developing child to secure his ego and be wild. Yet it is a period of life with no borders or understanding of others. In these early years of life, the prime saying of the youngster is "It's mine" or "I want it."

Mimicking the cosmic process of creation, where initially came *tohu*/chaos then *tikkun*/correction, a child, for the first few years of life, functions in a reality of tohu on all levels of existence, both in a state of chaos as well as being the source of chaos for others.

Cosmically, there is first the world of tohu then the world of tikun; "The Creator created worlds and destroyed them" *(Medrash Rabbah, 3; 7)*. The destroyed worlds are worlds of destruction, worlds of chaos and confusion. After the chaos, the "destroyed" worlds comes the world of *tikun*. Similarly, the development of a child moves from the destruction, egoic life of tohu to the constructive, orderly life of tikun.

The cosmic force of tohu is marked by ego, non-interconnectivity and non-responsibility. It is a reality where each dimension is on its own and there is no room for others or for any type of interplay. As a result, there is a meltdown of the world of tohu, and eventually there emerges a universe of tikun. Until three years of age children orbit in the world of self-absorbed tohu. There is no room for sharing toys or for understanding others. The way they see it, they need to spread themselves over as many things as possible, and claim everything in sight as their own. If such behavior would continue throughout life, if the ego were to never be checked or counterbalanced, there would ultimately be an external and internal meltdown.

Being of the world of tohu, the young child runs about wild, with long uncut hair. The child is hairy, much like the physical embodiment of tohu, the Biblical character Esav, the brother of Yaakov. The Torah relates that Esav was unusually hairy *(Bereishis 25; 25)*.

Now that the child has reached a ripe age of three, a haircut is due to facilitate movement into the world of tikun. We are born wild, and there can be no genuine spirituality or growth without structure, discipline and ethics. There must be a taming of wildness, a rectification of impulsiveness. The hair of the head will come to represent *sh'tus* /foolishness *(Medrash Rabbah, Bereishis, 11; 7. Mesech Chachmah, Kedoshim, 19; 27)* and the world of tohu, and thus needs to be cut occasionally.

UPSHERNISH

Getting a haircut in general and leaving the peyos, in particular, are symbolic representations of the movement into the world of tikun. A limit is set to the child's spreading out, and he moves into a level of maturity by taking the wild, untamed, undisciplined and chaotic consciousness of babyhood. Peyos set a physical and spiritual boundary to how much of the person extends outwards. At this point, the child has enough understanding and awareness of others that he can be educated and introduced to a more delineated, constructive tikun existence; a new life which includes beneficial order, egolessness and sharing.

The boundary of the peyos allows for greater integration, as the child begins to feel more secure in who he is and can then begin to appreciate others, as well. The more confident and loving a person is towards him or herself, the more appreciative and loving they can be towards others. In Hebrew, a haircut is called *tisporet*, from the root word *safar*, which also means boundary. This word is related to the word *sapir*, sapphire in English. From the boundary of the haircut and peyos, a new illumination arises, and the child shines brightly like a sparkling sapphire.

Peyos are generally formed in the shape of a line. The line of peyos symbolizes boundary and order. In addition to leaving peyos, upon the upsherin onward, the young boy is trained to wear tzitzis. Also called *talis katan*/small talis, it is a square garment with *dalet kanfos*/four corners, with eight strings hanging upon each corner. The garment itself is a square, another allusion to a line, or boundary. Yet there are a total of thirty-two strings that dangle from the corners, eight on each corner, symbolizing a penetration of the sharp edged corners and a downward flowing of energy. In its root the word tzitzis is connected with the word *nitzutz*/spark. As with tzitzis, sparks burst forth from the four corners and pierce through all squareness and the concept of being boxed in.

Besides the prominent imagery of lines and squares, the idea of tikun and order there is also a healthy counter-dose of circle energy, representing retention of tohu energy. If a line and a square represents order, boundary, finite, a circle represents transcendence, boundlessness, infinity. A line is defined with a clear beginning and end, not so with a circle which is undefined, with no beginning or end.

Peyos are lines, tzitzis is square, yet it is a corner garment from which energy flows outside of its parameters, albeit in the form of lines. More apropos is the donning of a *yarmulka*/headcovering, known as a *kipa*, on the head of the young child. Up until the boy was three years old, the boy went without a yarmulka, in fact, according to many traditions the boy should not put on a yarmulka, even temporarily, before the upsherin, and from this day forward the child puts on a yarmulka, a cap that covers the head, and as the head is round so too is the yarmulka.

There is an overall movement from the world of tohu into the world of tikun, from circle reality into line reality, from immaturity into maturity. Yet the purpose is always integration, to learn to move into the maturity of tikun without ever completely letting go of the passionate energy of tohu, to be responsible people without losing the almost simplistic joyful disposition of childhood. As we mature, we need to learn to channel "the Infinite Light, boundless energy of the world of tohu into the orderly vessels of tikun".

Chapter 6:

UNCUT HAIR
vs. NO HAIR

UPSHERIN IS THE CUTTING OF THE HAIR. TO MORE DEEPLY UNDER-
STAND THE NATURE OF THIS RITE OF PASSAGE, IT BEHOOVES US TO
EXPLORE THE ESSENCE OF HAIR. THERE IS MALE HAIR AND FEMALE
HAIR, AND WITHIN HAIR ITSELF THERE IS DARKER HAIR AND LIGHT-
ER HAIR, THERE IS HAIR THAT CURLS AND HAIR THAT IS STRAIGHT.
IN THE ZOHAR *(Idrah Rabbah, p. 129a)* EVERY STRAND OF HAIR IS
VIEWED AS HARBORING ENTIRE UNIVERSES, BUT WHAT EXACTLY
DOES THIS MEAN? WHAT IS UNIQUE ABOUT HAIR? AND WHAT DOES
HUMAN HAIR REPRESENT?

Before we can delve deeper into the nature of hair, understanding and deciphering the various forms of male hair (such as head,
facial and body) and female hair, we ought to first become famil-
iar with the way hair or the lack thereof is discussed in the Torah.

THE FIRST HAIRCUT

In the Torah we find that people committed to a life of holiness and service, as the tribe of Levi, needed to shave their hair completely, to initiate them into service *(Bamidbar 8; 7)* and the priests, the Cohenim among them were not allowed to grow long hair. The High Priest would cut his hair once a week and the other priests would cut their hair once a month *(Tannis, 17b)*. By contrast, the *Nazir (Bamidbar 6; 1-21)*, one who takes upon him or herself to be a Nazirite, "to separate themselves to G-d," to live a life of holiness, must never cut his hair. In fact, the hair is part of their holiness *(6; 5)*. The shaven hair of a Nazir is holy *(Pesachim, 23a)* and even needs to be discarded appropriately *(Temurah, 34a)*.

So there is an act of holiness in the context of long, unkempt, uncut hair, and holiness that demands the cutting of all hair.

Why the difference?

Traditionally, the Nazir is viewed as an ascetic. This is because a Nazir refrains from drinking wine, and simply allows his or her hair to run wild.

Gleaning through sources, it becomes apparent that most Nazirim in the times of the *Beis HaMikdash*/Temple times were young and single. As a means to fend off temptations they would move into the extreme opposite direction, and lead a life, most times it was temporarily, detached and removed from society.

The Nazir accepted upon himself to live a Nazirite life style as a spiritual retreat from the chaotic, aggressive and competitive nature of adolescence and youth. Struggling with life or being weighed down by negative temptations he or she wished to retreat and stand back, detach themselves from the pleasures of life, such as the drinking of wine represents, and also detaching themselves from life's sorrows, such as death, thus not touching or contacting the dead. They simply wanted to be, and observe, without too much participation in the drama of life, for better or worse.

Notwithstanding the positive role that being a Nazir could play in terms of healthy spiritual development, a Nazir represents a type of holiness and dedication that is not intended as a way of a structured life. Life in retreat is ultimately ego-based. In fact, the Nazir, after his stint as a Nazir needs to bring an offering of atonement, atoning for refraining from drinking wine *(Taanis, 11a)*. For the time being the life of a Nazir serves a wonderful purpose, a detachment to further a more focused meaningful involvement. Yet, life as a Nazir is meant as a time bound retreat, to transcend to later emerge and reengage with reality from a deeper perspective. It is a life of *pelah (Bamidbar 6; 2)*, which means detached, separate, and isolated, whereas life is meant to be lived, fully and with total mindful participation.

The polar opposite of the long-haired, poetically inclined, wild, free-flowing nature of the Nazir, is the Cohen, the priest, who served with little hair. This too is an extreme, with no ritual contamination and no hair. Though this life was the lot of an entire tribe, it also indicates a life detached from ordinary experiences; thus it was only one tribe's lot and not the entire nations focus.

In between the no hair and the long hair, is the short hair reality, which is relevant to all people and applicable to all times.

In the Torah we find the idea of having a haircut when a person comes before a king, as a sign of respect. *Yoseph*/Joseph was thrown into prison and when the ruler of Egypt heard of his amazing dream interpretation the verse says "Then Pharaoh sent

THE FIRST HAIRCUT

and called Yoseph, and they brought him hastily out of the dungeon; and he shaved himself" *(Bereishis 41; 14).*

In *halacha*/law the idea of having ones hair cut is a sign of respect, whether taking a haircut in the honor of Shabbos or the holidays, or any other momentous event *(Taanis, 29b. Moed Katan, 13a Yevamos, 43a).* The Medrash speaks of Rosh Hashanah/ The Day of Judgment as a time when we, in great confidence in the eventual outcome of the heavenly ruling, congregate, dressed in our finest attire, clean, and with our hair nicely trimmed *(Medrash Rabbah, Vayikra 29).*

As long hair or no hair represents a holiness that is detached from the everyday mundane reality, the balanced trimmed hair reflects the well-adjusted life of holiness; to live within world and yet to be above, to be above and yet enfolded within. In the words of classic Kabbalistic language, life is to be lived in a condition of *"Mati Ve'lo Mati/* touching and not touching" or "reaching and retreating". In fact, the only way to truly and fully be present in life is by remaining a slight measure above it, as the Kotzker Rebbe used to say, "If you wish to know the world, you need to soar above it".

Ultimately we express our full beingness when our lives mimic our Creator, when we are like our Creator, as it were, embodying both immanence and transcendence, being and non-being. On the one hand to be fully 'drawn within' world, not neglecting nor renouncing the beauty of creation or the value of this physical, and yet remaining somewhat above and transcendent of creation's trivialities.

A little boy until his ripe age of three, lives for the most part, a careless, selfish life, certainly not entirely interested or even equipped to participate as a fully integrated member of society. With his long flowing hair, his life of 'detachment' and 'non-responsibility' reminds us of the Nazir who also chooses to live detached and not responsible. Parents tend to shield their very young ones, and often for good reason, from the sorrows of life. In the same way, in joyful times children at this young age are apt to do their own thing and be in their own world.

And then the next stage of maturation begins, and the baby becomes a child. Borders of self-expansion are set and the child gets his hair trimmed. Mirroring the child's own development, the child begins to be more aware of others, and assumes more responsibility, the child is weaned from the cocoon of a protective home to a life within a greater society and school, through the cutting of the child's hair and leaving peyos. The cutting of hair indicates a movement from Nazir-like existence to a reality where the child can now fully, and with awareness, participate in the conversation of life.

Chapter 7:

THREE FORMS OF HEAD HAIR:
•DETACHED
•MASCULINE
•FEMININE

Exploring the Meta-Nature of Men's & Women's Head Hair

NOW THAT WE HAVE A BETTER GRASP IN THE WAY HEAD HAIR IS PRESENTED IN THE REVEALED ASPECTS OF TORAH, WE CAN COMFORTABLY MOVE INTO THE DEEPER DIMENSIONS OF TORAH, AND EXPLORE THE NATURE OF HAIR AND WHAT IT REPRESENTS.

Hair grows on mammals for protection to keep the body warm. On a literal level - the literal always being an outer reflection of the deeper - hair is threadlike outgrowth from our skin. Hair is present to protect the body's heat. For this reason hair is most present in the places of the body that have the most revealed life force, as the head. On a deeper level, hair is rooted in the space beyond the skin, as it were, beneath the surface of the epidermis. The intensity, measure and level of spiritual energy contained within a strand of hair depend on the interior beneath the surface from which the hair grows.

Overall, though hair is rooted in and nourished by the body, it contains little to no blood cells or nerves, and can thus be cut off with no pain.

As each strand of hair is thin and threadlike, and is not individually overwhelming. Hair reflects an energy flow that penetrates the below, the lower realms of reality, in a way that is measured and can be appreciated and appropriately accessed, as the word *sa'ar*/hair can be read as *shiur*/measurement. As such, flowing hair represent a flow of energy.

Beginning with hair of the head, there are three forms of such hair:

- In the language of the Kabbalah, there is the hair of *atik* / detached, removed, transcendent of all distinctions; which is part of the world of *keser*/crown, deep desire of reality; represented by the hair of the Nazirite, both male and female.

- There is the hair of *zeir anpin* (*z'ah*) / small face, hair of the male, masculine. zeir anpin is comprised of the six emotional Divine attributes, otherwise known as the emotional *sefiros*: *chesed*/kindness, *gevurah*/restraint, *tiferes*/compassion, *netzach*/perseverance, *hod*/humility and *yesod*/connection.

THE FIRST HAIRCUT

- The third is the hair of *nukvah*/receiver, immediacy, presence, feminine, hair of the female, feminine.

Essentially these are three types of head hair: one rooted in *atik*, another in *zeir anpin*, and a third in *nukvah*. Yet each one of these levels is considered an entire *partzuf*/structure on its own. There are a total of five *partzufim*, three of them are atik, zeir anpin and nukvah, the other two are *arich anpin*/long enlarged face, the idea of will and *a'v'a*/intelligence (combination of *Aba/Chochmah* and *Ima/Binah*). Each *partzuf* contains the entire arrangement of all the sefiros, albeit, occasionally in a *zeir*/smaller, contracted version so that each one is a total structure, a full Divine persona, as it were.

Think of the partzuf as a hologram, wherein each aspect contains the whole. For example, in the universe of emotions there is also intelligence, the intellect guiding and orienting the emotions; conversely, there are also emotions in the world of intelligence, as emotions stir and affect all intellectual understandings.

A cursory observation suggests that the actual hair on the head originates in the scalp. Metaphysically speaking, all head hair originates from within the skull. The deeper source of head hair is *"mosras ha'mochin/* "residue of the mind" *(The Maggid of Mezritch, Ohr Torah, 465. R. DovBer of Chabad, Imrei Binah, 2; 22c).* It can thus be called brain energy, or a surplus of excess brain energy.

From this perspective, the strands of hair serve as conduits or highways, carrying the energy of the brain into the surrounding environment. They also transport energy in the other direction, picking up subtle information from the surrounding environ-

UPSHERNISH

ment and feeding it to the brain.

The energy that flows from the inside out, from *mochin*/mind through each distinct strand of hair, is constricted and limited, like the actual thin shape of the hair itself. Hair contains a minutely thin measure of physical energy and thus can be cut with no pain. What is more, the life energy of hair is present within the actual *challal*/hollowed space within each strand. Accordingly, the *chayos*/life energy within hair is the least of the body's energy, even less than the life energy within nails.

Hair transmits and funnels energy, albeit condensed and contracted in its stream. Paralleling the cosmic structure, every strand of head hair, every blade of thin, linear hair represents a flow of *din*/ constriction and limitation, a fine condensed flow of light, as din is *tzimtzum*/contraction and concealment.

All head hair is rooted in 'excess mind'. Since *mochin* is a total partzuf with a full array of all aspects, within the hair of mochin there is hair that is connected with keser, hair associated with zeir anpin and hair related to nukvah. Since hair is normally associated with din and tzimtzum the act of trimming and shortening one's hair, both of the male zeir anpin and of the female nukvah, becomes a symbolic gesture. On a deeper level, an initiation of the trimming process dims and eliminates all manifestations of din and constriction in a person's life.

Though it is common for the head hair to be shortened, at least from time to time, the head hair of a Nazir is to remain intact as long as he or she is a Nazir. For the entire duration that a person accepts upon him or herself to live as a Nazir, the hair shall be allowed to grow as long as possible.

A Nazir, man or woman, is one who chooses to live for a period

THE FIRST HAIRCUT

of life detached and separate from social norms (this is different from the Nazir Olam / one who dedicates his entire life to this lifestyle). This reflects the Divine energy flow of *keser*/the crown, a space of transcendence, a place beyond the world of duality. And since there is "no left side [separateness/*Din/Kelipa*] in atik" *(Zohar)*, everything within atik/keser reality is *kedushah*/holy, enclothed within Divine Unity and plenty, the hair too of the Nazir is *kadosh*/holy, as in sublime and removed, and should not be tampered with or trimmed and allowed to grow long, as hair is generally a form of din and tzimtzum, the Nazir's hair is complete and absolute *rachamim*/Divine mercy. At this level of reality there is a radical transformation of the quality of hair, from Din - restrictions and confinements to *rachamim*/mercy and openness, and thus the hair is holy and should not be cut at all *(R. Yitzchak Chaver, Beis Olamim, 128b)*.

Though the condition of tzimtzum is non-existent in keser, and the hair of the Nazir is holy, still, the Nazir does have hair, which suggests some mode of *din*/restriction and concealment, as hair by definition is condensation and compression of energy.

Din and tzimtzum of the Nazir's hair is not related to the actual hair itself, so to speak; rather in the manner in which transcendent keser, beyond and above Infinite light is funneled and channeled into a finite creation, comprised of time and space.

There are two modalities of Hashem's Light that create and sustain creation. There is the transcendent Infinite light, the *ohr ha'sovev kol almim*/light that surrounds all worlds, and there is the imminent present light, the *ohr memale kol almim*/finite light that fills all creation. The Creator's reality makes itself manifest as both immanent and all-pervasive finite, as beingness form of life and as a light that is transcendent, infinite and beyond-being. Clearly, these images of surrounding and filling lights are not to be taken literally with spatial linear connotations, as they are both strictly relating to the degree of revelation and their observed presence within our reality.

Keser is the crown that hovers above creation, the infinite transcendent *sovev* light. The partzufim of zeir anpin and nukvah represent a more delineated, finite and invested form of enclothed *ohr*/light of *memale*/the 'fills' creation; zeir anpin as the light itself and nukvah as the actual embodiment of the light, and its presence within the physical.

In the world of memale, the drawing down, the progression of energy flow is *"B'derech Ilah V'alul*/in the manner of cause and effect"*. Since all are linked within a finite paradigm, albeit some more spiritually attuned than others, there can be an organic natural flow from highest into lowest, from cause into effect. In turn, the effect becomes the cause of another effect. Another effect, the movement of energy can follow a linear path.

With regard to the ohr/light of sovev / surrounds, however, getting from a point of infinity to a point of finitude, the *ilah v'alul*/cause and effect construct does not work; any quantitative evolution of infinity cannot produce finitude. A qualitative movement is needed, a quantum leap, a tzimtzum where the infinite retracts, as it were, and that is the drawing down *"b'derech sa'aros*/in a manner of hair"*, a revelation through the form of a tzimtzum, which now gives rise to the process of *ilah v'alul*/cause and effect.

When there is this little *ha'arah*/slim glimmer of these intense transcendent Infinite lights of Keser that become revealed in the form of b'derech sa'aros, a radical shift ensues. Originally being

THE FIRST HAIRCUT

the source the light of memale and eventually filtering down to become the light that is vested within finite creation.

As Nazirim are the living embodiment of keser, detachment, transcendent, beyond world, beyond Din and Tzimtzum, their hair is holy. Still, since keser lights are channeled into finite creation through sa'aros, they too have hair which represents restriction.

In the next chapter, the head hair and peyos of the male will be explored. For now, let us move from the Nazir, who can be either male or female, to the nature of non-nazir female hair. In truth, this topic deserves a book of its own, but to help better understand the idea of peyos and upsherin, we will touch upon the subject, albeit quickly.

The non-Nazir male, regardless of marital status, trims his (Zeir Anpin's) hair to lessen the aspect of Din and Tzimtzum and, traditionally, covers at least part of his head and hair with a form of headcovering, such as a kipa. On a deeper level, the purpose for this is to cover over his din. The laws and customs with regard to female Nukvah hair are much more intricate and complex.

In general, an abundance of hair represents an abundance of life-force and thus hair grows in the parts of body that have a more revealed life-force, such as the head. This relates to the inner reason of the tradition of women covering their hair when they are married. A primary gift a woman has is the ability to give birth to life *(Akeidas Yitzchak, Bereishis, Shaar 9)*. The original woman is both called *Isha/* woman and *Chava*/Eve. There is the definition of a woman as an Isha and there is the definition as a Chava. Chava comes from the word *Chaya*, 'life', as in "the Mother of All Life" *(Bereishis, 3; 20)*. When the word Chaya becomes a name, the letter Yud or 'Y' is exchanged for a Vav or 'V' *(Biur Hagra, Orach Chayim 5)*, and it becomes ChaVa. She is named 'Life' as she channels life into the world, and thus women are connected with hair, which is also a channel of life force.

There are various ways that hair covering is practiced today, ranging from wearing a scarf or hat to wearing a wig; some women even choose to wear a hat over their wigs. For technical and also practical purposes, married women tend to cut their hair shorter than before marriage; this is done for convenience, allowing them to feel more comfortable with a headcovering. With regard to a woman shaving her hair completely after marriage, this has become more obsolete in recent times. Within the Hungarian and Romanian communities, there are those who have the tradition to shave their heads completely. Yet many sages strongly discourage this practice.

There are two aspects to the act of married women covering their hair; one such aspect is modesty. Modesty should not be confused with shame or prudishness. It is an outward demonstration of not conforming to the objectification of women, and it directs others past the superficial qualities of the person to more essential qualities. This aspect of covering the hair is called "The way of the Jewish Women" or "The Way of Moshe".

Another purpose of women covering the hair is to cover over *din*/ judgment and not allow energy to flow to unwanted places. From the woman's perspective these two ideas are related. Here we are primarily exploring the first aspect of covering hair: covering or limiting the energy of din.

In general, the male hair (Zeir Anpin) is best trimmed short to negate *din*/constrictions and should be covered as well. This is regardless of a man's marital status. However, a married wom-

THE FIRST HAIRCUT

an's hair (Nukvah) need not be cut very short. According to most perspectives it should not be cut off completely, yet it should be covered.

Nukvah is the embodiment of the energy of memale/finite light, this light is tailored and perfectly fitted to the vessel (spiritual capacity), of the receiver. As the female reflects the energy and life force of this universe, the light of memale, eliminating all hair would cosmically represent a ceasing of all memale energy flow into this universe, a breakdown, as it were, in the process of creation.

There is cutting and there is covering; the difference between the two is that something cut is eliminated completely, while something covered is still present, just not observed by others. Hair that is cut off represents a total eradication of din, as the hair is no longer attached to its source of nourishment. Where din is still present with hair that is covered, but much less severely. The din is not available, as it were, for others to receive and others cannot be negatively affected by these dinim (the plural of din).

Traditionally, a non-Nazir male cuts his hair short and covers it, albeit often only some of the head and hair with a headcovering, as in a yarmulka/kipa; the married female does not necessarily cut her hair very short or shave; nonetheless, there is much greater stringency in regards to covering her hair.

For the male zeir anpin, there is more potential for an intense aggressive form of din -either within oneself or as expressed to others. Thus there needs to be a softening on all levels, both to cut and to cover the hair and to do so before and after marriage. The more genteel Nukvah is a reflection of the tender Divine memale energy enclothed within each minutia of creation, and manifests only according to the abilities of the finite receiver. Therefore, the Nukvah's hair can flow more freely before marriage, without a covering, and after marriage, protected under a covering.

The feminine is the embodiment of *Malchus*/the quality of royalty, receptivity, the feminine dimension of the *sefiros*, the Divine indwelling and presence within creation. Since this world is a place of din, with barometers and borders, the feminine which embodies the earth's and the world's energy could thus go with uncovered head hair before marriage, and afterwards, covered.

Prior to entering into an intimate relationship with another, a woman's heart and sensuality is private, closed-off. Entering into a relationship implies an opening and offering up of self, thus inviting vulnerability. With the ability to feel love and connect intimately with another person comes the possibility of hurt and heartbreak. Once the valve of giving and offering oneself to another is open, any parasite, as it were, can gain entry and receive sustenance from her. Being the embodiment of memale, a woman can wear her hair proudly for herself and for her husband, her beloved, without a covering. The enjoyment and nourishment her spouse receives from her tempered dinim are gentle, appropriate and properly directed to the receiver, but others, those who simply wish to prey on her openness and vulnerability, receive nourishment that is funneled towards *kelipa*/ unholiness, the shell which obscures the Divine beauty within everything.

Whenever there is a *yenika*/possibility for someone to receive nourishment from her in a positive form, in this case her spouse, there can also be a *yenika l'chitzonim*/spilling over of her energy to unwelcome outside forces. This is true on all levels, spiritually and physically, macrocosmically and microcosmically, when there is an opening of self to others, everyone can receive, both those who use this opening for positive purposes and those who use it for negative purposes. When there is a proper receiver, opening up and allowing others to enter can be greatly enriching to the person him or herself; and when there is not, it can be horribly devastating.

If a woman who has not yet entered into a sacred marriage relationship acts in a way that suggests wanting to be left alone and not desiring physically intimacy, there is little to no possibility for any type of yenika l'chitzonim. There is a closing off in this case, a shutting down of all yenika of sensuality. Once she enters into a physically intimate relationship in marriage, there is then an opening in the flow of this form of energy. Since she offers a holy yenika to her spouse, there can also be an unholy yenuka to kelipa, because hair, in general, and female's hair in particular, carries tremendous sensual energy. Kelipa, which is nothing more than an apparent concealment of Hashem's unity, cannot be nurtured or nourished in a place where there is no nourishment from kedusha/the holy. If, however, there is any opening for Kedusha, there can also be an opening for Kelipa.

To simplify, the reason there is a difference between head hair that is called kodesh/holy with no Din, as in the Nazir's hair, verses head hair that has din and thus needs to be cut and covered, as in the non-Nazir male hair, and hair that is longer and yet more strictly covered, as in a female hair, is determined by the spiritual root of the hair. When hair is rooted in atik/detached, transcendent space, as in the hair of the Nazir, who lives a detached existence, then there is no kelipa or din. Conversely, when hair is rooted in the male partzuf of zeir anpin or the female partzuf of Nukvah, there is potential for kelipa.

Chapter 8:

MALE HAIR

& THE ACT OF TRANSFORM-ING JUDGMENT INTO COM-PASSION

THERE ARE THREE TYPES OF ADULT MALE FACIAL HAIR:

1. Head hair
2. The beard
3. Peyos/sidelocks

These three types of male hair have different spiritual symbolism and qualities. There is hair that should be cut and covered; head hair; there is hair that should be allowed to grow, at least to certain lengths and does not need to be covered; the peyos, and there is hair that is not allowed to be cut, not even with a razor; the beard.

Being that this work is dedicated to the upsherin of a young boy, only the former two will be explored deeper, and facial hair will be discussed tangentially.

Head Hair:

Male head hair is associated with zeir anpin / small face; therefore, it needs to be cut and covered; ideally the majority of the center of the skull, so not to retain an excess of din. The act of cutting suggests a rectification, a tikun to the aggressive male quality, which is especially important to those male souls who are rooted in the root soul of *kayin*/Cain.

When any hair is removed, it is done with a razor, which is called a *ta'ar* in the Torah. The word ta'ar is spelled *Taf, Ayin Reish*. The letter Taf is 400, Ayin is 70 and Reish is 200; in total, the sum is 670, with the word itself equals 671. 671 is the same as the name *Ado-noi*/L-rd, Master.

The name Ado-noi is written with 4 Hebrew Letters, Aleph, Dalet, Nun and Yud. When each of these four letters is spelled out, the total number is 671:

Aleph is comprised of three letters: Aleph/1, Lamed/30, Pei/80 = 111.

Dalet is comprised of three letters: Dalet/4, Lamed/30, Taf/400 = 434.

Nun is comprised of three letters: Nun/50, Vav/6, Nun/50 = 106.

Yud, is comprised of three letters: Yud/10, Vav/6, Dalet/4 = 20.

Adding the totals together, 111 + 434 + 106 + 20 = 671.

As mentioned, male head hair represents din. When a person takes a *ta'ar*/razor - which reflects the Divine quality of Ado-noi - and cuts his hair, he sweetens and transforms the din of hair into a source of mercy, compassion and blessings.

Ado-noi is a Divine name connected with Hashem's attribute of indwelling within creation. The name Ado-noi is comprised of two words, Aleph and Din; so Ado-noi is Aleph Din/the One (the revelation of the Creator) within the Din. In the name Ado-noi, there is the element of Din / constriction and separation, and yet the Aleph, which is one and represents The One, is also present and revealed. Therein, there is an Aleph within din.

Through the act of the ta'ar, the name Ado-noi transforms Din into mercy. Generally, the name Ado-noi is one of transformation in that it takes the ineffable 4 letter Tetrgrammaton name of Hashem and transforms it into a name we can say; otherwise we are forbidden (nor do we know how) to pronounce this name. The name of Hashem is pronounced Ado-noi when making blessings.'

The beard:

With regards to the hair of the beard, the Torah tells us that we are not to eliminate these hairs. Our sages tell us this means it is

THE FIRST HAIRCUT

not permissible to cut the hair with a *ta'ar*/razor *(Makos, 20a)*.

The word for facial hair in the Torah is *zakan*. Zakan in numeric value is 157. The word zakan is spelled with three Hebrew letters: Zayin/7, Kuf/100, Nun/50 = 157. As we have a right and left side to the face we multiply zakan by 2 - 157 x 2 = 314. 314 is also the numeric value as the Divine name *Sha-dai*. The same Sha-dai is spelled three Hebrew letters: Shin/300, Dalet/4, Yud/10 = 314.

Sha'dai means enough *(Rashi, Bereishis, 17; 1)*. The Medrash *(Medrash Rabbah, Bereishis 5; 8)*, tells us that as the world was being created and endlessly expanding, Hashem said to the world *"Shad-dai/* Enough". Enough can also mean perfect; the facial hair is also perfect, with no Din.

Paradoxically, the word Shad-dai also denotes both an aspect of destroying, from the word *Shoded*/to break or destroy, and an aspect of nurturing, from the word *Shadayim*/the bosom, that which nourishes and nurtures a young suckling *(Shir Hashirim, 8; 1)*. Sha-dai is the Divine aspect that nurtures and gives life to creation. The name Sha-dai reflects itself in the ebb and flow of creation. Nature is continually creating and self-destroying, building and pulling down in one continuous rhythmic motion. There is constant movement fluctuating back and forth, but in all such movements, there is the guiding Divine nurturer protecting and allowing for further growth.

Beard hair represents this natural flow of creation and thus should be cut or tampered with to allow for this flow to occur naturally. Being a reflection of the natural flow of creation, the beard also comes to represent the Thirteen Attributes of Mercy, enumerated in the book of *Shemos*/Exodus *(34; 6-7)*, as in "Hashem, Hashem, (which are not counted as part of the Thirteen Attributes; *Maharal, Nesivos Olam, Nesiv Ha'Tefilah 6), E-l/*G-d, Merciful and gracious, slow to anger, abundant in loving-kindness and truth, remembering kindness..." and in the book of Michah *(7; 18-20)*. These thirteen qualities are not attributes of the Divine, rather attributes through which Hashem governs the world *(Morah Nevuchim, 1; 52. R. Menachem Rikanti, Vayechi. Shomer Emunim, 1)*.

In their higher form of revelation, the Thirteen Attributes are rooted in *keser*/crown, a space where there is no din, limits or boundaries, and so it, too, is holy as the hair of the Nazir and should not be cut. There is no reason to put a *ta'ar*, instrument of transformation, to the beard as the facial hair embodies the perfect quality of the Thirteen Attributes of Mercy, pure compassion and an Infinite Source for blessings, both spiritually and physically.

It should be noted that females can embody the structure of the lower part of these Thirteen Attributes of Mercy without the need for facial hair.

Peyos:

With regards to a boy having an upsherin, the head hair and the peyos are the most important to discuss here, as his head hair is cut shorter and his peyos are left.

Peah, as explained earlier, is the quality of Elokim (both peah, singular for peyos, and Elokim are 86 in numeric value), which sets borders and boundaries. Yet peyos are rooted in a very high spiritual place, even beyond the facial hair of the beard. The fa-

THE FIRST HAIRCUT

cial, beard hair is a reflection of the Thirteen Attributes of Mercy, which begins with E-l, however, both peyos, (one on each side), is rooted in the two names of Hashem, as in "Hashem, Hashem" that proceed E-l. The Thirteen Attributes begins with the word "*Hashem, Hashem, E-l*", yet the actual first attribute is E-l. Literally, where the peyos end, the facial hair of the Thirteen Attributes begins.

The hair of the peyos embodies both the quality of Hashem and Elokim and the unity between them, how the infinite transcendence of Hashem becomes manifest within the finite, bounded dimensions of Elokim, which is the place of din, time and space. The possibility for this unity of seeming opposites is because the peyos are rooted in "Hashem, Hashem," the Infinite, and on a deeper level, the Infinite and the finite are one.

Peyos are connected with the name Hashem, specifically how the name is revealed in it ability of *chiluf*/exchange. The name of *Yud-Hei-Vav-Hei*, in the exchange of *At-Bash* (where the first letter of the Aleph Beis becomes interchangeable with the last letter, and the second letter with the second to the last, and the third with the third to the last, and so forth) is Mem (for Yud), Tzadik (for Hei), Pei (for Vav) and Tzadik (for Hei). In numeric value, the name Mem/40 Tzadik/90 Pei/80, Tzadik/90 = 300.

300 is also the name Elokim in full numeric value. Elokim on its own is 86, as peah, yet when the letters of Elokim are filled, they equal 300. Elokim is spelled with five Hebrew letters:

Aleph/1, Lamed/30, Hei/5, Yud/10, Mem/40.

Aleph in full is Aleph/1, Lamed/30, Pei/80=111.

Lamed in full is Lamed/30, Mem/40, Dalet/4 = 74.

Hei in full is Hei/5, Yud /10 = 15.

Yud in full is Yud/10, Vav/ 6, Dalet/4 = 20.

Mem in full is Mem/40, final Mem/40 = 80.

111+ 74 + 15+ 20+ 80 = 300

Peyos are both *Elokim*/constriction and *Hashem*/Infinity, and the unity between them, the Infinite being infused within the finite. So while we generally need to use a ta'ar, which embodies the quality of *Ado-noi,* a transformative tool, and cut the head hair of the male, the peyos need to be left, leaving some space for din.

The peyos are much like a bridge between Infinity and the finite. Literally positioned between the head hair and the (eventual) facial, beard hair, the peyos serve as both a partition separating the negative hair from the positive hair, and the hair of pure din from the hair of the Thirteen Attributes of Mercy, as well as bridging the highest spiritual space into the lowest physical space.

Now we can better understand why the upsherin occurs at the age of three. Besides the fact that the age of three is a transitional period for a child, especially for a boy. On a deeper level, up until three, or thereabout, a child does not have the power to transform Din /judgment into *rachamim*/compassion. Transformation demands awareness and a heightened, evolved consciousness how to separate from certain ideas and how to integrate others. A young child lacks this discerning and *havdalah*/separating quality.

The fact that a toddler functions from a place with little or no sense of havdalah is connected with his inability to practice or perceive Havdalah, whether from his mother, and he generally does not yet have a sense of order where everything and every-

THE FIRST HAIRCUT

one belongs; so he wears his hair long. Upon transitioning from a toddler to a boy, which shows up as him being weaned from his mother, there is now a stricter sense of order, and the child begins to understand havdalah, individuation better. He begins to understand his place and his parents' place and others in his life.

Upsherin has traditionally become synonymous with Lag B'Omer / the thirty-third day of the Omer. This is because during the period of the Omer, from Pesach / Passover until a few days before Shavuos is a time of national mourning for the death of the 24,000 students of Rabbi Akiva and the cutting of hair is forbidden, except for on the day of Lag B'Omer. So any boy who turns three in that period can only cut his hair on that day. Also, the affinity between the two is related to the fact that one of the earliest sources of this custom is found in the writings of the Arizal, who took his young son on Lag B'Omer to Meron and gave him a haircut. On a deeper level, the haircutting and the day of Lag B'Omer are intricately connected.

The forty-nine days between Pesach and Shavuos represent forty-nine steps of personal development, progressing from the freedom experiences on Pesach to the assuming of responsibility of Shavuos, when we receive the Torah. This is a movement from a freedom "from" to a freedom "to"; a freedom to choose freely and responsibly the way of the Torah. There are the seven primary emotional *sefiros* /attributes and each of these attributes on its own without a healthy dose mixed in from the others creates a condition of *tohu*/confusion and chaos. To establish a tikun/correction and order, there needs to be a blending of the attributes so that each one of the seven contains all of the other, thus the sum total is forty-nine. Lag B'Omer is the day we celebrate both the passing of Rabbi Shimon Bar Yochai (one of the surviving students of Rabbi Akiva) and the day the students of Rabbi Akiva either ceased dying period, or did not die on that day. The thirty-third day of the Omer, which in terms of the Sefiros is either *Hod of Hod*/glory of glory, counting from the down up (from one to forty nine) or *Tiferes of Tiferes*/beauty of beauty, counting from the up down (from forty nine to one). Lag B'Omer embodies the quality of perfect tikun; as such, it is a most auspicious time to cut a young boy's hair.

Once a child is three and begins to leave the paradigm of tohu and enter the world of tikun, it is now the appropriate time to cut his hair shorter, leaving the peyos and setting boundaries and borders. At this transitional age we can begin to truly educate the child in the ways of mindfulness, order and discipline. Of course, coupled with measured discipline we must insure that the child continues to be treated with unconditional love and is given plenty of room for self-expression.

Chapter 9:

CUSTOMS OF THE UPSHERIN

&

THE ORDER OF THE CEREMONY

* The child is dressed in special clothes, wearing a Kipa (Yarmulka) and Tzitzis.

* A blessing should be made for the Tzitzis (if not yet said in the morning, when the Tzitzis were first put on). Standing up and wearing the Tzitzis the child should hold the Tzitzis (that is, the strings of all four corners) in his right hand (if left- handed, in his left hand) and recite:

UPSHERNISH

בָּרוּךְ אַתָּה יְיָ אֱלֹהֵינוּ מֶלֶךְ הָעוֹלָם
אֲשֶׁר קִדְּשָׁנוּ בְּמִצְוֹתָיו וְצִוָּנוּ עַל מִצְוַת צִיצָת.

(transliteration)

Baruch atah Ado-noi Elohei-nu melech ha olam, asher kid'sha-nu b'mitzvosav, v'tzivanu al mitzvas tzitzis.

(translation)

"Blessed are You, Ado-noi, our G-d, King of the universe, who has sanctified us with His commandments, and commanded us concerning the Mitzvah of Tzitzis"

After the blessing the child should kiss the Tzitzis, as is customary.

* Begin the Upsherin ceremony by offering a blessing to the child. The blessing should be offered by the parents, grandparents, as well as by a respected rabbinic figures.

* Many have the custom for a Cohen / member of the priestly tribe, to recite the priestly blessings:

יְבָרֶכְךָ יְיָ וְיִשְׁמְרֶךָ
יָאֵר יְיָ פָּנָיו אֵלֶיךָ וִיחֻנֶּךָּ
יִשָּׂא יְיָ פָּנָיו אֵלֶיךָ וְיָשֵׂם לְךָ שָׁלוֹם

54

THE FIRST HAIRCUT

(translation)

May Hashem bless you and guard you

May Hashem make His face shine on you and show favor to you

May Hashem lift up His face on you and give you peace

* The initial cutting of the hair is done ceremonially and in a festive mood.

* There are those who customarily begin to snip the hair from the place where the peyos grow, on the side of the head, to indicate that the specific purpose of the hair cut is to leave the peyos. There are others who begin the snipping from above the forehead, the place where the Tefilin will eventually be worn. Yet there are still others who begin snipping from the middle of the head, where the hair is most dense.

* There is a custom for a Cohen/member of the priestly tribe, to make the first cut; others reserve this privilege for an elderly rabbinic figure.

* Many begin with the father taking the first snip, as he is primarily responsible for the boy's education and is thus liable to leave the peyos. Afterwards, many continue with the mother, as the mother is traditionally the primary nurturer of a young child's development.

UPSHERNISH

* Other members of the family, if they wish, can also take part in the cutting, as well as friends of the family.

* When cutting the hair there are those that have the custom to recite the words of the verse:

לא תקפו פאת ראשכם

You shall not round the corners of your heads.

(Vayikra 19; 27)

* When taking a cut of hair offer the child a dollar or some change, to train the child in the Mitzvah of Tzedakah. The child takes the money and deposits it into a *pushka*/charity box that is next to him, so the child is giving Tzedakah at the ceremony.

* The money for charity is in addition to giving the child money or a gift upon this momentous occasion. The gifts leave the child with a positive feeling of his initiation into Mitzvos.

* While most people do the below at a later point in time, when they bring the boy for the first time to *cheder*/school, there is also a custom to take a sheet which the Aleph Beis written on it and cover the sheet with honey and have the child lick the honey. In this way, the Torah shall be to him "sweet upon his tongue".

THE FIRST HAIRCUT

* Our sages teach *(Sukkah 42a)* that from the moment a child learns to speak, his father should teach him:

תורה צוה לנו משה מורשה קהלת יעקב

"The Torah was transmitted to us through Moshe,
an inheritance for all the Jewish people"

(Devarim 33; 4)

These are the first words he should be taught to say. Many have the custom to recite this verse with the child at the celebration, as well as the verse of Shema;

שמע ישראל יי אלהינו יי אחד

"Hear Israel, Hashem is our G-d, Hashem is One"

(Devarim 6; 4)

* After the hair is cut, there is a custom to hide or bury it.

* A beautiful custom is to take the hair that was cut, weigh it and give the equivalent of its value in gold or silver to Tzedakah, charity. Many choose to give to charity related to the eventual education of the young boy such as a Yeshivah.

* During the ceremony, it is appropriate for someone to teach Torah.

* The ceremony is primarily an act of initiating the child into the world of responsibility and order, the world of Torah and Mitzvos, beginning with the child wearing a kipa and the garment of tztizis.

AFTERWORD

Having explored the deeper symbolism of hair and the purpose of the leaving of the peyos, it is our hope and prayer that very speedily we merit a time when "a star will arise from Yaakov... and burst through the peyos of the Moabite nation" *(Bamidbar 24; 17)*. Beyond the literal interpretation of this verse, this can also refer to the breaking of all boundaries and restrictions that limit our growth or integration.

Today, we need the element of din, albeit in a small measure, to insure the Divine flow of energy into our world. During our internal and external, personal and collective exiles we need a measure of constriction. Yet there will come a time when perception will be transparent, and a "star will arise...and burst through all limitations".

May we merit to observe the fulfillment of this prophecy speedily in our days, with the coming of Moshiach. Amen, may it be Hashem's will.

Addendum

THE THIRTEEN ATTRIBUTES OF MERCY

In the book of *Shemos*/ Exodus, after the episode of the Golden Calf, Moshe re-ascends to the Divine Presence to seek atonement for the people. "If you do not forgive them, wipe me out of this book", he declares. He goes a step further and asks to see Hashem's glory. Hashem says, "You will not see my face... but my back". As Hashem 'passes by', He reveals "The Thirteen Attributes of Mercy." Our sages envisions Hashem as wearing a Tallis, enwrapped in the Attributes *(Rosh Hashanah, 17b).*

The Zohar correlate these thirteen with a parallel thirteen

found in the Book of Michah. The Arizal correlates the Shemos attributes with the various parts of the Divine "Beard" (reflected in the human beard). The Arizal also correlates these attributes with the sefiros within keser.

Some sages say that the way to activate the attributes is simply by reciting them in a group, in a *minyan*. The Ramak argues that they must be actively embodied, and in his classic work *Tomer Devorah* he describes how to do this with regards to the Thirteen Attributes of Michah. He says a person should become like his Master. The Meor Vashemesh explains why we need to recite the Thirteen Attributes with a minyan. He suggests that since it is quite difficult to embody all thirteen attributes perfectly, by reciting them within a group of ten, it could be assumed that within the group as a whole there is a total perfection of all attributes.

Rashi (Ibid) begins counting from the name/attribute *Keil*. This perhaps implies that Hashem Hashem (usually counted as 1 and 2), here symbolize Divine Essence/*Atzmus*. The Thirteen are therefore revelations that flow from *keser*, Crown, which corresponds to the world of *atzilus*, the realmless realm of unmanifest manifestations of Essence.

Keser is above fixed categories of mercy and judgment. This reminds us that each of the Thirteen is inherently paradoxical. When to us it seems that the path of embodiment is unhealthy or merely "co-dependent enabling", we are forgetting that these are Divine Attributes within keser. We cannot approach them from a "victimized" or reactive or dualistic consciousness. Embodying them presumes self-mastery. Also, all of these embodiment practices are only real if they are done within the context of *halacha/* law. Halachically, we must act to prevent a violent person from hurting people, but this is putting Hashem's judgment into effect, not ours. We can remain merciful and positive. Theoretically then, we could actively embody forgiveness toward someone even while we are placing them in prison.

How do you become like your Master—how do embody keser? Through action. Attributes 1-8 are more revealed. As we rise higher and enter keser of kKeser, we begin to embody more interior attributes of Hashem, so to speak. Thus, 9-13 are similar to 1-8, but are more radically compassionate. The highest levels, the mind/*mochin* or *ChaBaD,* or ultimate reasoning of keser is not revealed. It is our mission to reveal the mochin of keser, and we do so through Torah.

SELECTED SOURCES
on the Attributes of Mercy:

* Hashem says, "You will not see my face... but my back." As Hashem 'passes by', He reveals "The Thirteen Attributes of Mercy" *Shemos 34; 5-7.*

* Hashem wearing a Tallis. *Rosh Hashanah, 17b.*

* The "Thirteen Attributes" as related in the Book of Shemos *(Shemos 34; 5-7)*: "Hashem, Hashem, Keil, Merciful and gracious, slow to anger, abundant in loving-kindness and truth, remembering kindness for thousands [of generations], forgiving iniquity and transgression and sin [of those who repent], but not clearing the guilt [of those who do not repent], passing along the sins of the fathers on the children to the third and fourth [generation]." The "Thirteen Attributes" as related in the Book of Michah *(7; 18-20)*: "Who is a God like You—Who bears transgression and pardons the wrongdoing of the remnant of His heritage. [He] does not sustain His anger forever, for He desires loving kindness. He will once more have compassion on us [and] forget our transgressions, and [He] will hurl all our sins into the depths of the ocean. [O God] grant truth to Yaakov [and] loving-kindness to Avraham as You vowed to our forefathers long ago."

* The Thirteen Attributes of Mercy from Shemos are the lower, while the Thirteen Attributes from the book of Michah are the

higher ones. They come from the place where there is no Din. *Zohar 3. p. 131a.* There are the Thirteen Attributes of *Arich Anpin*/Large Face, and the Nine Attributes in *Zair Anpin*/Small Face. *The Arizal, Shar Ha'kavanas. Derushie Chazaras Amidah 5. Eitz Chayim, Shar 13; 9-11.*

* These "attributes" are not meant to be understood as inherent qualities within Hashem, rather as the method of Hashem's activity, by which Hashem governs the world. *Rambam Moreh Nevuchim, 1; 52. R. Menachem Rikanti, Vayechi. Shomer Emunim, 1.*

* According to many of the *mekubalim*, *(R. Bachya, Shemos 34; 7. R. Eliyahu Di Vidas, R. Moshe Alshich. Bamidbar 14; 20)*, simply reciting the Thirteen Attributes is not sufficient, one needs to embody and emulate these attributes in his relationships with others, and then they have power. The Ramak explains how we are to embody these qualities. *Tomer Devorah.* The Ma'or Va'shemesh explains that this is the reason why we can only recite the Thirteen Attributes with a Minyan, a quorum of ten men, since if it is difficult for one person to always embody all these qualities, in the group, we can assume all these attributes are present. Yet, there are other sages who say that the way to activate the Attributes is simply by reciting them. *Safer Hafla'ah. Bnei Yissachar, Mamorei Elul. Maamor 2:4.* Clearly, as the Maharal explains, for them to be effective we need to recite them with proper intention and focus.

SELECTED SOURCES

In Hebrew the haircut is called *tisporet*. Many Arabic speaking Jews call this celebration *chalkah* – from the Arabic word *lakya* for haircut. *Note Bereishis 27; 12 where the word chalak refers to a lack of hair.*

The Ari went to the gravesite of Rabbi Shimon Bar Yachai with his child Moshe to give him a hair cut on the thirty third day of the Omer. *Shar Ha'Kavanos Inyan Pesach Derush 12.* This is clearly an older custom, as R Chayim writes *"minhag yaduah/a known custom".* *Note: Teshuvas Radbaz 2, Siman 608.* According to strict *halachah*/law a child, even today, can have a haircut on the day his born, certainly if the hair is getting in his way. *R. Chayim Kanevsky Sha'alas Rav 1; 15. p. 72.* Yet, the *minhag* is to wait, certainly according to Kabbalah.

Being that the hair cutting ceremony is a joyful occasion, many have the custom to play music at the celebration. *Sdei Chemed Asifas Dinim, Maareches Beis Ha'Kneses, Os 10.*

Early sources write that the first cutting is allowed from when the child is 13 weeks. Others speak of when the child is nine months. Or when the child is 2 years. Or even at 4 years. *Leket Yosher Hiechal Avodas Hashem 2, p. 179. Teshuvas Peulas Tzadik. 3, Siman 236. (Note Rashi Berieshis 21; 8.) Keser Shem Tov (Gagin) 1-2. p. 591. Igros Kodesh. Vol. 11.p. 60.* In Talmudic times, and apparently in times prior there was no custom as to when to cut the hair, in fact occasionally the baby's

THE FIRST HAIRCUT

hair was cut when he was yet a small infant. *See Moed Katan 14a.*

Three is the age Avraham became aware of the Creator. *Nedarim 32a. Tanchumah, Vayera 22.*

The letter *gimel* in the word *VaHisgalach/*and he shall shave *(Vayikra 13; 33)* is large. Perhaps hinting to the cutting of the hair at the age of three, as the letter *gimel* is the number equivalent of three. Also, when it says with regards to Yitzchak, that Avraham "made a great feast the same day that Yitzchak was weaned". *Berieshis 21; 8.* The word the Torah uses for weaned is *va'yigamel* which phonetically is related to the word gimel, the third letter in the *Aleph Beis*, which represents the number three. Though the *pasuk/*verse is speaking about a celebration on Yitzchak's second birthday, after twenty four months. *Rashi ad loc. See also Shemuel 1. 1; 24.*

Orlah is not allowed for the first three years. Kabbalistically this has to do with impure spirits that are attached to the trees for the first three years. The first three years is 'the three impure Kelipos.' *Zohar 2. p. 244b. Sharei Orah Shar 5. Pardas Rimonim Shar 24. Likutei Torah, Kedoshim 29c.*

The parallel between Orlah and hair cutting is a relatively new insight, though there are traces for this comparison in the Talmud. *Yerushalmi peah, Chap 1; 4. See also: Tanchuma, Kedoshim 14. Chidushie Ha'Ritva, Shavuos in the beginning. See: Shu't Arugas Ha'bosem. (Hungarian) Orach Chayim, Siman 210.*

The parallel between hair and trees is found in the medrash. "He

UPSHERNISH

created within man everything that He created in the world. He created forests in the world and forests in the body, and that is hair. *Avos D'rebbe Nason, 31; 3.*

The Medrash speaks about four forms of Orlah. *Medrash Rabbah. Bereishis 46;* 5. Orlah of the "ears" *Yirmiyahu 6; 10.* Orlah of the mouth. *Shemos 6:30.* Orlah of the heart. *Yirmiyahu. 9; 25. (See: also Devarim. 10; 16.)* And the Orlah of the body *Bereishis, 17; 11.*

For a parallel between peyos and peah. *See: Ohr HaTorah (Tzemach Tzedek) Vayikra (Hosafos) p. 322.*

The main purpose of the first upsherin is the leaving the peyos. *Sharei Teshuvah Ohr HaChayim Siman 531; 7.* Also for the purpose is to educate the child. Also, his first cut is like *Reishis Ha'gez/*first cutting. *The Lubavitcher Rebbe Likutei Sichos Vol. 7 p. 351.*

Until the age of the first haircut, there are some who in fact dress the boy in more girl like clothing. This was the custom of the Jews of Yemen. *Yehudi Teiman, p. 147.*

"*U'bar Yerech Imo*"/"the fetus is as one of the limbs of the mother", according to *R. Eliezer Chulin 58a.* Interestingly, R. Yoseph Engel brings down that a man is called a father at the moment of conception, whereas the women is not considered a "mother" until she gives birth. She becomes a mother at birth, until then the child is still part of herself. *Beis Ha'Otzer, Erech Av.*

THE FIRST HAIRCUT

"Isha K'man De'mahila Dami"/"a women is like circumcised" *Avodah Zarah 27a.* Perhaps, with regards to girls the more dramatic transitional age is a bit later in life, much more pronounced at the time of maturity, the time of the Bas Mitzvah (12 years), in addition, the transition from a pre-gender to gender is not as drastic for the young girls, as the mother, traditionally is the prime care taker.

Tzitzis is similar to hair, and brakes the negative Kelipa identified with hair. *See Likutei Halachos. (R. Nason of Breslov) Hilchos Tzitzis, Halacha 4.*

The Zohar views every strand of hair as harboring entire universes. *Zohar 3, Parshas Naso Idrah Rabbah 129a.* Every strand of hair is a distinct conduit of energy, shaped as the letter Vav, the letter that connects. *R. Chaim Vital. Shar Ha'Mitzvas. Parshas Kedoshim.* Hashem says "I have created many hairs in a man's head and for every hair I have created a separate follicle" *Niddah 52b. See also Shaloh, Shar Ha'Oysyos, Oys Kuf, Kedusha 2.*

The Zohar elaborates on the various different colors of hair, the lengths, density and so forth and connects them with the various personalities of people. *Tikkunei Zohar Tikkun 70.*

The Levites cut off their hair completely when they were initiated into service. *Bamidbar 8:7.* The Priests were not allowed to serve with long hair. *See Taanis 17a.* Yet, as the Zohar notes "The holiness of the Cohen is connected with their hair. *Zohar 3, Parshas Naso p. 127a.*

A king needs to cut his hair every day, whereas the high priest once a week. *Ibid.* The Talmud speaks of a particular hair cut the high priest/*Cohen Gadol* would take. *Sanhedrin 22b.* There were Talmudic sages that would take the same style hair cut. *Shabbos 9b.*

The Nazir's hair is holy. *Pesachim 23a.* And when cut their hair should be burnt or in other situations buried. *Temurah 34a.*

There are three prohibitions upon the Nazir, not to drink wine, not to impure him or her self, and not to cut the hair. Whether the Nazir is one that does these three, and the 'doing' creates the holiness, or, conversely, a Nazir is one that accepts upon himself to be more 'holy' and as a result does not violate these three prohibitions is debated.

Additionally, the question is whether these three have the same implications. Is the holiness the not drinking wine, and thus, the result not to cut the hair, or, is the Nazir who does not drink wine and grow his hair. The Rambam asserts that the *mitzvah* of a Nazir is to accept upon himself to grow his hair and not to drink wine. *(Safer Hamitzvos Mitzvah 92)* while the Chinuch writes *(Mitzvah 374)* the Nazir is one who refrains from drinking wine, and thus the mitzvah is that he should grow his hair. According to the Rambam, the actual idea of Nazir is to not shave and not drink wine. While the Chinuch holds, that the holiness of the Nazir is that he chooses not to drink wine, and as a result such a person does not shave his or her hair. *Avnei Meluim Siman 15, and Siman 22.*

Traditionally an excess of wine is seen to lead to sin, thus " One who sees a wayward wife in her state of degradation should prohibit himself from wine" *Sotah 2a.*

Most Nezirim were single. With regards to the Nazir the verse says, "to his father or mother, brother or sister he should not defile himself" *(Bamidbar 6; 7)* Why not mention his children as it says with regards to a Cohen? *(Vayikra. 21; 2)* That is because most of them did not have yet children, as they were single. *R. Yaakov Kamenetzki. Emes L'Yaakov, Nosa. p. 223.* Josephus writes of the custom among single men to become Nezirim. *Josephus, Against Apian Book 2. Chap 25. Note: Amus Chap 2; 11.*

Going with long hair creates humility. *Rabbeinu Bachya, Bamidbar 6; 2.* And shows a disgust for matters of the body. *R. Tzadok of Lublin, Poked Akarim 4.*

Nazir as a sinner, for refraining from wine. *Taanis 11a. Note: Yerushalmi End of Kedushin.*

Yoseph trimmed hair in honor of the king. *Bereishis 41; 14. See also: Megilah 16a.*

UPSHERNISH

In honor of Shabbos one should take a haircut. *Tannis 29b. Yevamos 43a.* Also in honor of Yom Tov. *Moed Katan 13a.* With regards to Rosh Hashanah, *see: Tur Orach Chayim Siman 581. Medrash Rabbah Vayikra. Parsha 29. See also: R. Yitzchak Abuhav Menoras HaMaor Ner 5 Klal 2, Part 1, Chap. 1; 5. p 291* regarding the beard.

The sages tell us that a king should cut his hair each day. Why should a king to cut his hair every day? R. Abba Ben Zavda said, this is because, as the Torah says, "Your eyes shall see the king in his beauty". *Tannis 17a.* So in general a cut head of hair is considered for a man more beautiful. Yet, *see Rambam Madah, Hilchos De'as, Chap 4, Halacha 19. Kli Yakar, Bereishis 25; 25.*

Hair of Atik, Zeir Anpin, and Nukvah. *Ta'amei Hamitzvos Parshas Kedoshim.* Certain hair is holy and certain hair can be the source for a *Yenikah L'Chitzonim. Derech Mitzvosecha, Mitzvas Tigalachas Metzorah. See also: Ohr Ha'Torah, Parshas Emor, p. 588-93.*

Nazirs hair is the source of *memalah*, the light of *sovev. Likutei Torah Parshas Emor 32a.*

There are two aspects to the covering of the male head; one is the issue of "respect" sensing the One above, the other is related to covering of *din*. Already in Talmudic times the custom was for men to cover their heads, as the Gemara says; "Rav Hunah the son of Rav Yehoshua would not walk four cubits bareheaded, saying: The Shechinah is above my head" *Kedushim 31a. See also Shabbos 118b. Meseches Sofrim, 14: 15.* (Though note; *Nedarim 30b.* "Men sometimes cover their heads and sometimes do not, women's hair is always

THE FIRST HAIRCUT

covered, and children also go bareheaded"). From the above sources it appears that the wearing of a headcovering is merely an act of Chassidus –piety. Yet, the Beis Yoseph understands the wearing of a headcovering, outside as an obligation, (certainly today) and not merely an act of extra measure of piety. *See Perisha Orach Chayim 2; 6. See also Taz with regards to today. Taz Orach Chayim 8:3. Igros Moshe Orach Chayim, 1; 1. Note: Zohar Parshas Balak.*

There are also two aspects to women covering her hair; one is the issue of Tznius –modesty, inwardness, either because of *Da'as Moshe* or *Da'as Yehuudis*, and the other the issue of *din* and the *yenika*/drawing forth to "outside forces", though with women these two issues are related. The idea of inwardness and modesty is not to be viewed as an expression of submission or shame, rather as a symbol of resistance to the commodification of the body, an act of liberation. The Mechaber rules that women "both married and unmarried *(i.e.; once married, Chelkak Mechokek, Beis Shmuel, Dagul Me're-vavah, ad loc.)* should not go out in the marketplace with their heads uncovered." *Even Ezra, Siman 21; 2.* The Levush quotes the words of the Mechaber and adds "and there is a deeper meaning according to Kabbalah". The entire conversation in this work on upsherin is with regards to covering male and female hair strictly from the point of view of hair as din, not dealing with the issue of Tznius. Clearly the other issue for males need to also be taken into consideration, as for example, a hairless male should still wear a Kipa.

With the female the idea of *tznius* and *din* are more interrelated. Thus in a world of perfection and Unity, if there was absolutely no *yenikah* to outside forces than perhaps there would also be no issue with hair and tznius, as it says with regards to Adam and *Chava*/Eve in the Garden of Eden; "And they were both naked...and were not ashamed" *(Bereishis 2; 25). (Note also with regards to the Cohen viewing the uncovered hair. Bamidbar 5; 18. Sotah 8a).* We find regarding *Olam Habah*/the perfect world to come that the prophet predicts; "Then...and from the streets of Jerusalem the voice of joy and the voice of gladness, the voice of the bridegroom and the voice of the bride." *(Yirmiyahu 7:34)* Or as Zecharyah says; "Old men and old women will yet sit in the streets of Jerusalem" (8; 4.) Though, generally *Kol Isha*/sound of a woman singing is *Erva* as hair, *Berachos 24a,* and there is still a need for separation in the earlier stages of Moshiach, *Sukkah 52b,* yet these prophecies are talking about *Olam Habah (Tosefos Makkos 24b),* which is the most perfect, integrated, unified state possible.

Hair comes from *Mosras Ha'Mochin*/residue of brain", and their *hamshacha*/drawing down is not by the way of "cause and effect." *R. DovBer of Chabad Imrei Binah 2, p. 22c.*

With regards to shaving the head completely, it appears that in Medieval European Jewry it was the common custom, until it was forbidden by a decree of the Czar in 1851. The custom remained in places in Eastern Europe which were not under Russian rule, such as Hungary and Romania. Yet, in the Torah shaving off all the hair for a woman was viewed as rendering the women less attractive. *Devarim 21: 10-14. Rashi ad loc.* In fact, the Gemarah speaks of the Creator grooming *Chava's*/ Eve's hair and then presenting her to Adam. *Berachos 61a. Eiruvin 18a. Nidah 45b.* The Arizal teaches that a woman should not cut her head hair completely. *Shar Hamitzvos*

THE FIRST HAIRCUT

Parshas Kedoshim. Shulchan Aruch Arizal, Siman 181:1. Similarly, the Lubavitcher Rebbe strongly discourages the shaving of the head completely. *Sha'arei Halacho U'Minhag Vol. 4. p. 141. This is (Note regarding long hair. Eiruvin 100b. Note: Pesachim 110a.)* With regards to *nukvah* and hair on the other parts of the nukavah's body *see: Sanhedrin 21a, Rashi. Gittin, 6b. Note also Pesachim 43a.* When *Keneses Yisrael* (whom Nukvah is an embodiment) is in an elevated state then there is no *kelipa* (hair) surrounding the body. *Rabbi Yoseph Caro Magid Mesharim Parshas VaYigash.* The Zohar speaks of the cutting the hair of the body of nukvah before the *yichud* with *duchrah. Zohar 3, p. 79a. Parshas Emor. Zohar 3, Parshas Naso, p. 127a.*

Shaving the head completely is seen in the Torah as an act *nivul/* distastefulness. *Devarim, 21; 12 Rashi. However, the Ramban, ad loc,* views the act of cutting off the hair as an act of mourning. *See also: Rambam. Morah Nevuchim, 3:41.* The prophet Yirmiyahu says: "Cut off your hair, O Jerusalem, and throw it away, and take up a lamentation on the high hills...*(7; 29)* Interestingly, the halacha is that a mourner is not allowed to cut his hair. *Meod Katan 14b.* Shaving all the hair was also done, in certain situations as an act towards purification. *Vayikra 14; 9.*

The Ben Ish Chai writes that since hair of a woman is connected with din, thus when a woman braids her hair she should have in mind that she is uprooting and minimizing all din. *Ben Yehoyada, Berachos, 61a.*

Hair carries sensual energy, and thus can become a source for

UPSHERNISH

Yenika to inappropriate Kelipa vessels. (This Yenika is available to Kelipa when there is a Yenika for *Kedusha/* her spouse. When there is no Yenika to Kedusha there can be no Yenika for Kelipa. *Hosafos. Likutei Sichos. 23, Parshas Nasso. Likutei Torah Vayikra 24a. 32a.)* Though normally this negative potential refers to female hair, *Berachos 24a,* male hair that is worn in a particular fashion can also be a source of Kelipa. *Zohar. 1. p. 166b. Tanya. Kuntras Acharon, 5. See also: Kedushas Levi Parshas Yisro p. 99. See Rosh Hashanah 26b. Note Sotah 9b with regards to Avshalom.*

There is a Torah prohibition against the total elimination of facial hair. *Vayikra 19; 27. Makos 21a. Torahs Kohanim Parshas Kedoshim, 6; 4. Kidushin 35b.* The sages tell us that this means with a *Ta'ar/* Razor. *Makos 20a.*

With regards to the Name *Sha-dai see: Medrash Rabbah Bereishis 5; 8.*

The "Thirteen Attributes" as related in the Book of Shemos *(34; 5-7):* ("Hashem, Hashem,) "E-l, Merciful and gracious, slow to anger, abundant in loving-kindness and truth, remembering kindness for thousands [of generations], forgiving iniquity and transgression and sin [of those who repent], but not clearing the guilt [of those who do not repent], passing along the sins of the fathers on the children to the third and fourth [generation]." The "Thirteen Attributes" as related in the Book of Michah *(7; 18-20):* "Who is a God like You—Who bears transgression and pardons the wrongdoing of the remnant of His heritage. [He] does not sustain His anger forever, for He desires loving kindness. He will once more have compassion on us [and] forget our transgressions, and [He] will hurl all our sins into the depths of the ocean. [O God] grant truth to Yaakov [and] loving-kindness to Avraham as You vowed to our forefathers long ago."

Thirteen Attributes of Mercy from the book of Shemos are the lower Attributes, whereas the Thirteen Attributes from the book of Michah are the higher. They are rooted in Keser, a space where there is no Din. *Zohar 3, p. 131a.* Certainly, these "attributes" are not meant to be understood as inherent qualities within Hashem, rather as the method of Hashem's activity, by which Hashem governs the world. Rambam *Moreh Nevuchim, 1: 52. See also: R. Menachem Rekanti Parshas Va'Yechi. Shomer Emunim Part 1.*

There is great debate in Halacha whether the prohibition for the male to cut the facial hair is limited to a Ta'ar or a similar tool, but not for example with a scissor, or whether it extends to any form of cutting. From a Kabbalistic perspective the facial hair should not be cut at all.

The Medrash writes that the hair on the head grows "with stupidity" whereas the hair of the beard grows "with cleverness". *(Bereishis Rabbah, 11; 7. Mesech Chachmah, Kedoshim, 19; 27).* This is connected to *Mochin* / mind and even beyond Mochin, *Keser.* The male beard, *Diknah* is connected with the "thirteen attributes of mercy". *Zohar 3 (Parshas Nosa Idrah Rabbah) 131a.* Though this concept seems related only to males, (who have beards) in truth it is also related to females. In general, in *Kisvei Arizal/* the writings of the Arizal it says that Malchus has no Diknah. Yet, in *Shar HaKelalim p.*

41, it is written that Malchus does have Diknah, (not Diknah itself, as women generally do not have facial hair), rather, the place of the Diknah. R. Moshe Chaim Luzzato (the Ramchal) elaborates on how within the Nukvah of Leah there are six *Tikunie Diknah* and how on the level of Rachel there are four Tikunim. The Ramchal also said that the main purpose his soul came down to this world was to reveal this truth.

There are thirteen attributes in Arich Anpin and nine attributes in Zeir Anpin. *Eitz Chayim, Shar 13; 9-11.*

The Torah and the sages do not offer a specific measurement of how many hairs need to be left as peyos. The Rambam writes there should be a least 4 (or 40) hairs. *Rambam Hilchos Ak'um 12; 6. (Kapach)* The Shulchan Aruch rules that the entire space on the side is considered peyos. *Yorah Deah, Siman 181; 9. See also: Shar HaM-itzvas (Arizal) Parshas Kedoshim.* The length of the peyos is (at least) until the edge of the lobe of the ear. *Shulchan Aruch Ibid.* The Arizal, as an adult would cut his peyos once they reached the hair of the beard. *Shar Hamitzvos Ibid. Shulchan Aruch Arizal, Siman 181; 2. See also: Beis Lechem Yehudah Yorah Deah 181; 1. Darchei Teshuvah Ibid. 17.*

The two peyos are rooted in the "Hashem, Hashem" before the Thirteen Attributes of Mercy. *R. Tzvi Elimelech of Dinav Bnei Yissaschar Mamorei Chodesh Elul 2:2.*

The peyos are the *Parsah*/partition between the ten Sefiros as they are within *Galgaltah*/crown of the head, -i.e.; hair of the head, and the thirteen attributes of mercy, i.e.; facial hair. *The Rebbe Rashab, Hemshech Ayin Beis Vol. 2. p. 952-961.*

Many have the custom to have the Upsherin in a Shul/ synagogue. *See Sdei Chemed. Asifas Dinim. Maareches Beis Ha'Kneses Oys 10.*

Regarding bringing a child into Cheder and covering the Aleph Bet with honey and having the child lick the letters, see *Kav Ha'Yashar Chap 72, p. 245.*

With regards to weighing a child's hair and giving to equivalent to charity. *Teshuvas Radbaz 2, Siman 608.* Note *Yumah 38a* with regards to a mother weighing the child and giving the equivalent of gold to the Temple. We do find in Tanach that hair was weighed, with regards to Avshalom. "But in all Israel there was none so much praised as Absalom for his beauty...And when he shaved his head...because the hair was heavy on him...he weighed the hair of his head at two hundred shekels according to the king's weight. *Shmuel 2. 14: 25-26. See Ralbag ad loc.*

One the child is three years old we ought to teach them the verses of Torah of "Shema Yisrael..." and "The Torah was transmitted..." See also; *Ohr Hachayim, Vayikra 19. Note: Sukkah 42a* regarding a father teaching his child the verse of Shema and the verse "The Torah was transmitted..." The simple meaning in reference to Shema is the Mitzvah of reading Shema, that the father should teach his child to say the Shema. Rashi, however, understand that there is no Mitzvah to teach the child how to say the Shema. *Rashi, Berachos*

UPSHERNISH

20a. Rather the saying of Shema is part of educating the child in the Mitzvah of learning Torah. *See also: Biur Ha'Grah, Shulchan Aruch, Orach Chayim, Siman 70. See also Hilchos Talmud Torah Admur Ha'Zaken 1:1.* From the time of the Upsherin we should educate the child in the wearing Tzitzis, morning blessings, blessings (before) and after eating, and the saying of the Shema before going to sleep. *Hayom Yom, Daled Iyyar.* With regards to Tzitzis *see: Kitzur Shaloh, Inyanei Tzitzis.*

OTHER BOOKS BY
RAV DOVBER PINSON

Rav Pinson's books are widely available in bookstores, as well as online at **www.amazon.com**

REINCARNATION AND JUDAISM
The Journey of the Soul

INNER RHYTHMS
The Kabbalah of Music

MEDITATION AND JUDAISM
Exploring the Jewish Meditative Paths

TOWARD THE INFINITE
The Way of Kabbalistic Meditation

JEWISH WISDOM OF THE AFTERLIFE
The Myths, the Mysteries & Meanings

THIRTY – TWO GATES OF WISDOM
Awakening through Kabbalah

UPSHERNISH

THE PURIM READER
The Holiday of Purim Explored

EIGHT LIGHTS
8 Meditations for Chanukah

THE IYYUN HAGADAH
An Introduction to the Haggadah

THE MYSTERY OF KADDISH
Understanding the Mourner's Kaddish

RECLAIMING THE SELF
The Way of Teshuvah

PASSPORT TO KABBALAH
A Journey of Inner Transformation

THE FOUR SPECIES
The Symbolism of the Lulav & Esrog

A BOND FOR ETERNITY
Understanding the Bris Milah

THE FIRST HAIRCUT

THE GARDEN OF PARADOX:
The Essence of Non Dual Kabbalah

BREATHING & QUIETING THE MIND
The Jewish Meditation Series

MYSTIC TALES FROM THE EMEK HAMELECH
Adapted, Explained and with Commentary

VISUALIZATIONS & IMAGERY
Creative, Imagery & Awareness

WRAPPED IN MAJESTY
Tefillin- Exploring the Mystery

INNER WORLDS OF JEWISH PRAYER
A Guide to Develop and Deepen the Prayer Experience

ABOUT THE AUTHOR

Rav DovBer Pinson is a world-renowned Torah scholar, prolific author and beloved spiritual teacher.

He is widely recognized as one of the worlds foremost authorities and communicators of authentic Kabbalah and Jewish philosophy.

Through his books, lectures and seminars he has touched and inspired the lives of thousands the world over, and continues to serve as a mentor to many across the globe.

He has authored over 25 books, many of which have been translated into various languages, such as Hebrew, German, Spanish, Russian and Portuguese.

Rav Pinson is the Rosh Yeshivah of the IYYUN Yeshiva and Dean of the IYYUN Center in Brooklyn, NY.

THE FIRST HAIRCUT

UPSHERNISH

www.ingramcontent.com/pod-product-compliance
Lightning Source LLC
Chambersburg PA
CBHW030500100426
42813CB00002B/296